# STONES
# IN HIS POCKETS

Photo: Nobby Clark

MARIE JONES

# STONES
# IN HIS POCKETS

Introduction by
Mel Gussow

**APPLAUSE**
NEW YORK • LONDON

*Stones in His Pockets* first published in the U.S. in 2001 by Applause Theatre & Cinema Books

ISBN: 1-55783-472-5

*Stones in His Pockets* first published with *A Night in November* in Great Britain in 2000 as a paperback original by Nick Hern Books Limited

Lines on p. 41 from 'Whatever You Say, Nothing', from *Opened Ground*, by Seamus Heaney, quoted with permission from Faber and Faber Ltd and Farrar, Straus & Giroux in the USA

**Library of Congress Cataloguing-in-Publication Data**

Library of Congress Card Number: 2001088727

**Amateur Performing Rights**   Applications for performance in excerpt or in full by non-professionals in English throughout the world should be addressed to Nick Hern Books, 14 Larden Road, London W3 7ST, *fax* +44 (0) 20-8746-2006, *e-mail* info@nickhernbooks.demon.co.uk

**Professional Performing Rights**   Applications for performance by professionals in any medium or in any language throughout the world should be addressed to Ben Hall, Curtis Brown Ltd, Haymarket House, 28-29 Haymarket, London SW1Y 4SP

APPLAUSE BOOKS
151 West 46th Street
New York, NY 10036
Phone: 212-575-9265
email: info@applausepub.com

SALES & DISTRIBUTION
HAL LEONARD CORP.
7777 West Bluemound Road
Milwaukee, WI 53213
email: info@halleonard.com

*Stones in His Pockets* was first performed in Belfast at the Lyric Theatre on 3 June 1999, and was staged at the Tricycle Theatre, London, in August 1999. It opened at the New Ambassadors Theatre, London, on 24 May 2000, with the following cast:

JAKE QUINN . . . . . . . . . . . . . . . . . Seán Campion
CHARLIE CONLON  . . . . . . . . . . . . . Conleth Hill


*Director*  . . . . . . . . . . . . . . . . . . . . Ian McElhinney
*Set Designer* . . . . . . . . . . . . . . . . . . . Jack Kirwan
*Lighting Designer*  . . . . . . . . . . James C. McFetridge


It opened in New York at the Golden Theatre, 252 West 45 St. on April 1st, 2001, with the following cast:

JAKE QUINN . . . . . . . . . . . . . . . . . Seán Campion
CHARLIE CONLON  . . . . . . . . . . . . . Conleth Hill


*Director*  . . . . . . . . . . . . . . . . . . . . Ian McElhinney
*Set Designer* . . . . . . . . . . . . . . . . . . . Jack Kirwan
*Lighting Designer*  . . . . . . . . . . James C. McFetridge

Produced by Paul Elliott, Adam Kenwright, Pat Moylan, Ed and David Mirvish, and Emanuel Azenberg/Ira Pittelman.

INTRODUCTION

By MEL GUSSOW

In *Stones in His Pockets*, a Hollywood movie is being
filmed in a  small sleepy village in County Kerry,
Ireland, and two local men are among the many who
have been cast as extras. If that sounds like an
unpromising idea for a play, you have not seen Marie
Jones's delightful comedy, which recreates the filming
and the town — pub, parish and farmland. On its most
immediate level, *Stones in His Pockets* is a performance
piece for actors, as Conleth Hill and Seán Campion dart
in and out of 15 roles. With a slight shift in manner, ges-
ture and costume, they play Charlie Conlon and Jake
Quinn who in turn become a cross-section of characters,
those from Hollywood as well as those from Ireland
(almost all of whom seem to be distantly related). The
virtuosic actors imitate the stuffy English director of the
film, the flighty American star and her entourage, assis-
tant directors, extras, hangers on — the diverse popula-
tion of a movie on location.

Having seen Hill and Campion when they first brought
the show to the Tricycle Theater in London in 1999 —
before it moved into a long run on the West End and
then to Broadway — I cannot imagine anyone else playing their roles. The playwright freely acknowledges that
they have been integral to her creative process. But
other actors are doing the play in theaters around the

world, and many more will do it, as it becomes a perennial. It must be remembered that *Stones* is first of all a play, a text for performance. Reading it after seeing it is its own joyful experience, and it also acts as a kind of clarification. Onstage, some of the transformations flash by so quickly that even the most alert theatergoer may miss a switch. Read it and savor Ms. Jones's own virtuosity.

What begins — and continues — as a sharply satiric portrait of filmmaking, the crotchets, customs and egocentricities of artists in action, soon becomes a full vivid landscape of this corner of Ireland. Subtly the playwright offers commentary on the Hollywood invasion, the susceptibility (and the shrewdness) of the natives and the universal craving for a chance to stroll in the spotlight. Hollywood may be a corruptive influence, but there are those who are eager to be exploited. The subtext of the play is, in the author's words, "the whole disintegration of rural Ireland."

One of the most incisive characters is Mickey Riordan, who boasts of being the last surviving extra on "The Quiet Man," the seminal Hollywood-in-Ireland movie. "Wee Mickey," as John Wayne called him, he has cadged drinks and made a career out of his brief cinematic exploits. Other locals know better than to encourage his long-winded reminiscences. But he is also the savviest of the extras on the new film (a period romance called, significantly, "The Quiet Valley"). He knows that once scenes have been shot, he and the others are "in the can," and cannot be fired. As he says,

"It will luk bloody daft in the last scene if the whole lot of us luked like a whole load of other ones."

On the production side there is the careless dialect coach. When the star, Caroline Giovanni, has trouble with her Irish accent, he tells her not to worry because "Ireland is only one per cent of the market." Therefore, what price authenticity? At the center, of course, are Jake and Charlie, Jake who has had a short and very unsuccessful stay to New York, and Charlie, the former owner of a failed video store, who has a movie script in his back pocket. Jake has come back home with the notion that he might become a film star. Instead, as an extra he is relegated to digging turf as a "background bog man." Invited by the flirtatious star to visit her at her hotel, Jake decides he will win her favor by pretending to be a poet. When asked to deliver a sample of his writing, he borrows a verse from Seamus Heaney. Caroline, who has done her homework, immediately spots the source and also corrects Jake's misquote. Sheepishly he responds, "It always works on Irish girls."

Underlying the comedy is the poignant story of Sean Harkin, a dreamy local lad who is tossed out of the pub by the leading lady and is thereby subjected to a public embarrassment in his hometown. Depressed, he drowns himself. As the parish priest says, "Imagination can be a damned curse in this country" — imagination and ambition. As Jake tells off Caroline, "You come here and use us, use the place and then clear off and think about nothing you leave behind."

Moviemaking has long been a subject for films, from *Singin' in the Rain* through François Truffaut's *Day for Night* to David Mamet's *State and Main*, a film that shares a sensibility with *Stones in His Pockets*. But it has been far less prevalent in the theater. There is, of course, one other recent Irish example, Martin McDonagh's *The Cripple of Inishman,* in which a young man hopes to be in Robert Flaherty's *Man of Aran.* For one thing, it is difficult to simulate the expansiveness of a film on stage, a challenge Ms. Jones overcomes by simplification.

Clearly she knows the territory. She is not only the author of 27 plays (including "Women on the Verge of HRT"), she is also an actress who has experienced the pleasures and trials of working in movies on location in Ireland, most notably with Daniel Day Lewis in *In the Name of the Father.* In her own way, she is moviestruck, and enjoys acting in a film and making money while being pampered for a week's work. Fortunately, she has retained her objectivity and her sardonic perspective. She knows that there is "frustration in the Irish acting community," in which professionals can be reduced to being extras and she also knows the effect a film can have on its location. That effect can be immediate (a village's single policeman who has never seen live cars in any one day is suddenly directing motorcades of traffic) and long-range (the village where *The Quiet Man* was filmed is still on the tourist map).

In its earliest form, the play was presented with Hill and another actor by the Dubbeljoint Theater Company in Belfast. Then with Campion joining Hill and directed by the author's husband Ian McElhinney, it opened at the Lyric Theater in Belfast. After a tour, it moved to the Tricyle in London — and went on and on. Ms. Jones gives full credit to her creative team (the director and the actors), saying, "I have no visual eye whatever. I had no idea how I would have staged it. In a funny way, it's like radio: nothing there but words and a few signs." The scenery is minimal: a trunk, a line-up of shoes to represent the ensemble of characters. But despite the author's disclaimer, the play is sharply focused and also has wide peripheral vision. It was, of course, her inspiration to have it interpreted by two actors. For the playwright, that approach is nothing new. For economic as well as artistic reasons, she has often asked actors to double in roles in her plays. In *A Night in November,* about the conflict between the Irish Republic and Northern Ireland, one actor is called upon to play 25 characters.

*Stones in His Pockets* has been a phenomenal success, winning the Olivier Award as Best Comedy in London, and being produced in Australia, Iceland, Sweden,

Germany, France and other countries. Naturally the question arises if the play will come full cycle and be filmed. The movie rights have been sold and, from the first, the idea was to film it with a complete cast of actors. Ms. Jones seems sanguine about the possibilities (though she was not interested in writing the screenplay) and allows herself one thoughtful observation. In a twist of fate, movie stars will undoubtedly play the roles of extras. As for the author, she will continue to concentrate on playwriting. For Marie Jones, imagination is, of course, a blessing not a curse.

—Mel Gussow
*March, 2001*

Photo: Nobby Clark

# STONES
# IN HIS POCKETS

## Characters

CHARLIE CONLON, *mid thirties*

JAKE QUINN, *mid thirties*

CHARLIE *and* JAKE *play all the other characters in the play:*

SIMON, *first A.D.* (*Ambitious Dublin 4 type*)

AISLING, *third A.D., young, pretty, anxious to impress those above her, no interest in those beneath*

MICKEY, *a local in his seventies, was an extra in* The Quiet Man

CLEM, *the director, English, quiet nature, not much understanding of the local community*

SEAN, *a young local lad*

FIN, *a young local, Sean's friend*

CAROLINE GIOVANNI, *American star*

JOHN, *accent coach*

BROTHER GERARD, *local teacher*

DAVE, *a crew member, Cockney*

JOCK CAMPBELL, *Caroline's security man, Scottish*

## Setting

*A scenic spot near a small village in County Kerry*

## ACT ONE

CHARLIE *stands front stage as if queuing up at a catering truck.*

JAKE *is lounging in the sun.*

CHARLIE. I'll have the lemon meringue pie please . . . I know I was up before but it's not for me . . . it's for my mate . . . yes he is, he is an extra I swear . . . he can't come and get it himself because he has just sprained his ankle . . . okay . . . (*To man behind him.*) don't shuv there's plenty left . . . (*To* CATERER.) an accident report sheet? . . . he only went over on it, it's not life threatening . . . no he doesn't want a full dinner he only wants the sweet . . . (*To man behind him.*) I know we are only meant to have one helping but it's not for me . . . (*To* CATERER.) Look, I don't know why he can eat a sweet and not his dinner if he's sick, what am I a doctor or something . . . the fella asked me to go and get him a helping of lemon meringue pie . . . fine fine . . . No problem. (*Walks away.*)

Jesus Christ the Spanish Inquisition to get a bloody pudding.

JAKE. They've got wise to the extras . . . first couple of days ones were bringing their families down and feeding them too . . . (*Laughs.*) My mate has sprained his ankle . . . not very good was it . . . have you Ballycastle men no imagination . . .

CHARLIE. How do you know I am from Ballycastle?

JAKE. You were in the pub last night talking to a few of the locals . . . small town, word gets round . . . Jake Quinn . . . how are you doin' Charlie.

CHARLIE. What is this, the caterer gettin' on like he was trained by the R.U.C. and you by the Special Branch . . . no fear of gettin' homesick anyway.

JAKE. How did you end up here.

CHARLIE (*furtively looks around him*). You mean you don't know . . . was there a break down in intelligence?

JAKE. You're very jumpy.

CHARLIE. Have to be man . . . I'm on the run.

SIMON. Aisling, get this lot back to work. Use a cattle prod if you have to. What about these catering vans?

AISLING. Just moving them now, Simon. Thank you. (*Gesturing to vehicles.*)

SIMON. I'm going to get Miss Giovanni from her Winnebago now.

AISLING (*third A.D.*). Quiet everyone settle . . . please finish your lunch quickly before we lose the light . . . the next shot is a close-up on reacting to you . . . then we will turn the camera and have you reacting to Maeve . . . remember what you are reacting to . . . Maeve is telling you she will plead your case to her father . . . remember your positions exactly and those of you who were wearing caps . . . please put them on.

CHARLIE (*to* JAKE). Was I wearing a cap, I can't remember.

JAKE (*smirks*). So you're on the run then.

CHARLIE. Keep your voice down.

JAKE. On the run.

CHARLIE. Aye.

JAKE. On the run from who?

CHARLIE. The Boys . . . understand.

JAKE. Jesus . . . no messin'.

CHARLIE. Aye they weren't bad though, they give me a head start . . . they says Charlie, we will close our eyes and count to twenty and you run like the hammers . . . I thought that it was very dacent.

JAKE (*to* CHARLIE). You don't have to tell me if you don't want to . . . only making conversation.

CHARLIE. Aye, sorry mate, it was the lemon meringue pie interrogation that got to me . . . well I am on the run, sort of . . . had a video shop that went bust . . . them Extra Vision bastards . . . I never heard one person in Ballycastle complain to me before them hures opened up . . . you know . . . if a video was out the customers would take something else, no problem . . . the big boys move in and gullible Charlie here thinks . . . my customers are loyal.

JAKE. Look out, here she comes . . . You were just in front of me beside oul Mickey and you had your hat on.

CHARLIE. Sure it doesn't matter.

MICKEY. Oh it will surely matter, they will check thon Polaroid and see for sure who was wearing what and you don't want to be gettin' yourself in trouble with your one with the yoke on her ear . . . you have to keep your nose clean for thon one has a gob on her that would turn milk.

CHARLIE (*puts his cap on*). Happy now, Mickey?

MICKEY. Not me fella, I'm only warning you, if you

don't want to be replaced you do as you're bid . . .
just say nothin' and you will be forty quid a day the
wiser, that's my motto Jake.

JAKE. Aye right Mickey.

CHARLIE. Right pain in the ass.

JAKE (to CHARLIE). My mother's third cousin. Do you
know that man's famous. He's the last surviving
extra on *The Quiet Man* . . . but don't get him started. Where were we . . . aye the Extra Vision hures.

CHARLIE. Aye . . . I says to myself . . . they won't
desert me . . . my customers won't desert me . . . I
am one of them, support your own and all that . . .
fuck was I wrong . . . (*Mimics them.*) Charlie you
have to have more than two copies of a video, Extra
Vision has loads . . . Charlie you want to see the
range Extra Vision has . . . then they stopped saying
anything 'cos they just stopped coming . . . so I got
up one morning, . . . all my plans for the future in a
heap of out-of-date movies . . . I couldn't start all
over again . . . started all over again so many times
I've lost count . . . this time I just couldn't do it . . .
so I closed the door on the shop . . . videos still on
the shelves, nothing touched . . . threw the tent in
the boot and decided to do Ireland . . . what about
you.

JAKE. Well I can't follow that.

CHARLIE. Ah don't mind me . . . just thought I would get it all out at once, save the locals making it up for me . . . oh and the other thing, my girlfriend dumped me too . . . talk about kicking a man when he is on the floor . . . and you'll not believe this.

JAKE. She is going out with the manager of Extra Vision.

CHARLIE. How did you know?

JAKE. You told the story last night in the pub to a second cousin of mine.

CHARLIE. Jesus, that's me and gin . . . bad combo . . . anyway, the place is coming down with Hollywood stars . . . it's a who's who of who's bonked who, and me, Charlie Conlon is a topic of conversation . . .

JAKE. We are used to that lot . . . it's outsiders coming in and taking jobs we don't like.

CHARLIE. Place is coming down with outsiders . . . it's like a bloody circus . . . there she is . . . look . . . me, Charlie Conlon only ten feet away from Caroline Giovanni . . . I'd give her one alright.

CAROLINE *and dialect coach.*

CAROLINE (*as she crosses*). Can I try the other earrings? These are too dingly, dangly. (*Practises.*) I will speak to my father, you have suffered enough.

JOHN. You're doing great Caroline . . . remember always to soften the a; and elongate it . . . I will speak to my father, you have suffered enough.

CAROLINE (*she repeats badly*). I will speak to my faaather, no . . . I will speak to my fetherr . . . shit . . .

JOHN. No Caroline put your tongue behind your teeth.

CAROLINE. Thaaather.

JOHN. No . . . No, your bottom teeth.

CAROLINE. Faaather . . . fetthe . . . fatttther . . . shit . . . these people will think it sounds ridiculous.

JOHN. Don't worry . . . Caroline . . . Ireland is only one per cent of the market.

CAROLINE. I want to get it right John.

CHARLIE (*to* JAKE). I love that, huh . . . half of America here is playing Irish people and they say I am the outsider.

JAKE. They promised the extras would be local . . . she is gorgeous.

CHARLIE. I got it fair and square . . . saw the Ad, extras wanted and they liked the look of me . . . pitched my tent and here I am . . . great money and free grub . . . it's a gift . . . Would you . . . you know, give her one?

JAKE. No chance of getting near her.

SIMON Right, let's go for this now. Good morning, Caroline, looking lovely this morning, love those earrings.

AISLING. Simon will I bring Rory out yet?

SIMON. No . . . it's bloody freezin' . . . he will go crazy hangin' about.

AISLING. Does Maeve not need to see him . . . you know the big moment of electricity.

SIMON. No . . . he comes over the hill just as she turns away from the mob. It's the next shot (*Flirting.*) silly girl.

AISLING. I'll go get his blankets . . . and have him stand by.

SIMON. Hey Aisling.

AISLING. Yes Simon.

SIMON. What do you call a Kerryman with brains?

AISLING. I don't know Simon.

SIMON. Dangerous.

*They laugh.*

AISLING. I don't get it Simon.

SIMON. You will Aisling, you will.

CHARLIE (*to* JAKE). What are we supposed to do?

JAKE. Look at her lookin' at us looking dispossessed.

CHARLIE. Dispo what?

JAKE. Like this. (JAKE *demonstrates.*)

SIMON. Happy to go Caroline. Turnover, Speed, mark it
   alright Clem, ACTION.

*They look dispossessed, music plays.*

SIMON. Cut . . . beautiful Caroline . . . Stay in your
   places 'til we check the gate. Someone get Caroline
   a cup of coffee.

JAKE (*to* CHARLIE). Terrible bloody accent.

CHARLIE. Doesn't matter . . . been that many film stars
   playing Irish leads everybody thinks that's the way
   we talk now . . . I have my own film here . . .

JAKE. A Film?

CHARLIE. Yeah . . . I sat in my shop day after day
   watching movies and I says to myself . . . Charlie,

you could do that so I did . . . here it is . . . and here I am right smack in the middle of the people that can make it happen . . . I'll choose my moment and wey hey.

JAKE. I'm impressed Charlie.

CHARLIE. Don't grovel, you will have to audition like the rest.

CAROLINE. It's not right John . . . I want it to be right . . . the rhythm is wrong.

JOHN. Fine let's go to the pub the night . . . mix with the locals . . . get a feel.

CAROLINE. Yeah . . . yeah I will . . . I think I would quite like that.

JOHN. . . . but be careful Caroline, you can't be too exact, you won't get away with it in Hollywood, they won't understand.

CAROLINE. Hollywood is shit John . . . a crock of shit . . . look around this place . . . god it's just heaven on earth . . . I love this place . . . I'm third generation you know, on my mother's side . . . I do get a real feeling of belonging here you know that. You people are so simple, uncomplicated, contented.

CHARLIE (*to* JAKE). It would founder you up here. That wind would cut the arse off ye.

JAKE. Be a while yet, have to turn the camera on us.

CHARLIE. So then it's us lookin' dispossessed, luking at her with loads of land.

JAKE. Nah, it's not us they want it's the Blasket Islands.

CHARLIE (*looks around*). Bloody amazing.

JAKE. Yeah . . . they'll get a big shot of the Blaskets and the peasants, then Rory comes over the hill behind us like he is walking out of the sea. When he has his line, the lot of us disappear, even the Blasket Islands.

AISLING (*second A.D.*). Quiet everyone . . . settle . . . that's a wrap for the extras . . . we will pick this up tomorrow afternoon . . . quiet settle . . . I want all the extras in the turf-digging scene in costume by seven a.m. tomorrow morning . . . and make sure you leave all costumes in the Community centre . . . don't be tempted to go home in them . . . quiet . . . settle . . . that is all the men in scene 37 . . . tomorrow at seven a.m . . . breakfast will be from six.

CHARLIE *has his script in his hand.*

CHARLIE (*to* AISLING). Excuse me.

AISLING (*stops him with her hand as she speaks into her walkie talkie*). . . . Hi Simon . . . Yeah Kurt is mad we're not getting to his scene . . . he was psyched up for it . . . right will do . . . cheers Simon.

CHARLIE. Excuse me . . . (*She stops him from speaking.*)

AISLING. Come back, come back, come back. Listen carefully everyone . . . slight change of plan you will be picked up at six-thirty a.m. tomorrow and taken to the location by minibus so that means everyone in costume by six . . . the minibus will leave from the community hall sharp at six-thirty . . .

CHARLIE. Excuse me.

AISLING (*sharply*). Yes.

CHARLIE *bottles out and puts his script back in his pocket.*

CHARLIE. Are the ones in the Turf diggin' scene the same ones as the ones in the cart the day?

AISLING. Well where was the cart going?

CHARLIE (*blank . . . looks around for support . . . but no-one else seems to know*). I don't know.

AISLING. Taking the men to dig the turf . . . (*Stops him again.*) . . . Hi Simon . . . right . . . (*To* CHARLIE.) Excuse me.

*She leaves.*

MICKEY. Don't start gettin' yourself noticed . . . just
keep your head down and go where they put you . . .
that's how to survive as an extra.

CHARLIE. It's the gettin' up at the scrake Mickey is the
killer.

MICKEY. Sure what would you be going to bed for if
you have to be up for the scrake?

CHARLIE. Aye dead on Mickey . . .

MICKEY. And don't be going home in them boots . . .
the continuity would cut the heels off you.

CHARLIE. I'll remember that Mickey.

MICKEY (*to* CHARLIE). Do you know I'm famous as
I'm one of the few surviving extras on *The Quiet
Man* . . . John Wayne called me by my first name
. . . he would always refer to me as wee Mickey.

CHARLIE. Did you call him Duke?

MICKEY. No I did not, I give the man his place . . . I
mind one day.

JAKE. Hey Mickey there's the forty quid man comin'.

MICKEY (*to* CHARLIE). I'll catch you later.

JAKE. He will spend that in the pub and by the morning he will owe twenty more and the morra night he will pay back the twenty straight off and by the end of the night the same thing . . . I don't think that man's liver could survive another movie.

*SFX Interior changing room . . . showers running etc.*

*They start to undress and get into their day clothes during the following dialogue . . .*

CHARLIE. Have you done this before?

JAKE. No but most of the town have, there was another big movie a few years back . . . the locals have got cute to it now . . . a woman that runs a guest house in the town had all her rooms full for the first time ever, a whole summer with a no-vacancies sign up, she was delighted with herself . . . this year she and her family are sleeping in a caravan at the bottom of the garden . . . she let their rooms out too . . . last time they loved the glamour and the attention with a few bob thrown in . . . this time it's the money and the money and the money . . . sad.

CHARLIE. Sad? . . . now hold on a minute . . . me going bust to Extra Vision is sad . . . somebody making twice what they made last year is not sad . . . you miffed cause you didn't get a part last time . . . not luk Irish enough.

JAKE. Nah I was in the States.

CHARLIE. What did you do there?

JAKE. This and that . . . you know bit of this bit of that . . . worked a few bars, waited a few tables.

CHARLIE. Not make your fortune.

JAKE (*sarcastically*). No, came back here to be a film star.

CHARLIE. Tell ye what, this is the life.

JAKE. A background bog man . . . dead glamorous.

CHARLIE. You have to start somewhere, if you keep your nose clean there could be a nice wee part in mine . . . could you handle a sub machine gun . . . ?

JAKE *mimes sub machine gun action.*

CHARLIE. Don't call me, I'll call you.

JAKE. You haven't a hope Charlie, it's who you know in this business, . . . that Aisling one, you know the one with the Walkie Talkie grafted onto her ear . . . she is for the top that one . . . Father is a director, wants to produce her own films . . . and she will.

CHARLIE. I suppose it wouldn't even cross her mind that she might not.

JAKE. Definitely not.

CHARLIE. She is only about twenty.

JAKE. Makes you sick.

CHARLIE. Yeah but if you've got it, doesn't matter if you're a nobody . . . talent is talent . . . it wins through in the end.

JAKE. You don't believe that do ya . . .

CHARLIE (*sharply*). This is Charlie's day of good cheer, nothing or nobody is going to put me in Joe Depressos.

JAKE (*taken aback*). Wouldn't dream of it . . .

CHARLIE. Jesus . . . look at that young fella, he has lost it.

JAKE. That's Young Sean Harkin, a second cousin of mine . . . drugs . . . pain in the arse . . . I'm off to the Jacks.

SEAN. Jumped up tart . . . jumped up fucking tart . . .

CHARLIE. Hey mate, settle yourself.

SEAN. That hure, who does she think she is . . . I need a job.

CHARLIE. Well look at the state of you, this is big

money, they can't take a chance on an extra messing
it up.

SEAN. I was fucking born diggin' turf and that hurin'
slag is tellin' me to piss off.

CHARLIE. She does have a point you know.

SEAN (*turns on him*). And who the fuck are you Mr
Brown Noser.

CHARLIE. Nobody . . . just, an extra.

SEAN (*as he staggers off*). You're a nobody, just like
me and she won't give me a job.

JAKE. Is he gone?

CHARLIE. Yeh. Come on Jake, I need a drink.

JAKE. Aye, with you in a minute. Hey Fin, you're his
mate, can you not talk to Sean?

FIN. He came yesterday, but he was out of it and she
told him to clear off. He was alright this morning
and he asked me to put his name down. I told him to
be here for two o'clock and he would get a start, but
for fuck sake look at him.

JAKE. What's he on Fin?

FIN. Whatever he can get his hands on.

JAKE. Can ye not do something, say something . . . he is killing himself.

FIN (*exiting*). And say what, I mean what would you say Jake, don't do them nasty drugs, and get a life?

CHARLIE. Come on Jake. Are you alright?

JAKE. When he was a young buck, he used to look up to me, his Da's farm was next to ours . . . followed me everywhere . . . Come on Charlie, I need that drink too.

CHARLIE. Don't let me drink gin . . .

*Bar scene . . . background Country and Western music.*

JAKE. Another gin there Kevin and a couple of pints . . . business is boomin' then Kevin . . . a restaurant? . . . sure you wouldn't get many in this town atin' out when they cud ate in . . . of course the place will be comin' down with tourists after this one . . .

SEAN *staggers up to* CHARLIE.

SEAN. Hey Brown Noser, have ye anything on ye . . . I can pay.

CHARLIE. Piss off Sean.

SEAN. Please mate.

CHARLIE. I have nothin', clear off.

SEAN. Yis all think yis are movie stars, yis are nothing, I'm Sean Harkin and I am a somebody and I fuckin' know yis are all nothin' . . . wankers.

CHARLIE. Away home son, your Ma wants ye.

SEAN. Tossers . . . fuckin' tossers . . . full a shit.

*He staggers away from him . . .* CHARLIE *looks at him, for that brief moment . . . but doesn't want to think about it.*

JAKE. How is it goin' Sean, . . . look at him, seventeen and out of his head . . . keep thinkin' I should have a talk with him . . . (*Distracted.*)

CHARLIE (*a bit pissed*). . . . You know mate I was so depressed . . . so depressed . . . I just couldn't even lift my head . . . you know it just gets to you physically like . . . I luked at myself in the mirror and I says . . . Charlie you have lived on this planet for thirty-two years and what have you to show for your existence . . .

JAKE. Maybe you should go on the pints man.

CHARLIE. Sorry mate . . . yeah stop this . . . no, this is Charlie's day of good cheer. So, this woman in America, did she dump ye?

JAKE. Nah she wanted to marry me . . . an ultimatum
. . . I couldn't do it . . . I could just about look after
myself . . . Me stuck there with a wife and kids to
support and not a clue about the future . . . a mate of
mine went over the same time, he's got a wife and
two kids . . . he works two bars and a late night
restaurant . . . what kind of life is that . . . so here I
am on the dole and back living with the ma.

CHARLIE. Jesus look who is sitting in that corner.

JAKE. Caroline Giovanni . . . when did she come in?

CHARLIE. Mixing with the plebs . . . I tell you there is
not a man in here wouldn't give her one.

JAKE. There is not a man in here would get a look in.

CHARLIE. She might you know . . . for research pur-
poses . . . could be trying for a taste of the real
thing.

JAKE. You've sex on the brain man.

CHARLIE. It's not my brain that's the problem . . . Jesus
look at the cut of Kevin the owner he is practically
salivating.

JAKE. You know what he will do, he will get the wife
to make her a sandwich and when the restaurant
opens he will have a big plaque saying . . . Caroline
Giovanni dined here . . . I was right, there's Bridget

haring off into the kitchen.

CHARLIE (*watching her go*). Go on ye girl ye.

JAKE. Jesus man look at her, she is so sexy.

CHARLIE. Bridget? . . . It's a gas . . . did you ever think you would be sittin' in the same pub as Caroline Giovanni . . . hey luk she is eyeing you up . . . or is it me . . . (*Moves across the stage and realises she is still watching* JAKE.) No, fuck, it's you . . .

JAKE (*shouts*). No, I have a pint on order thanks . . . yeah it's great . . . that was a lovely scene today . . . very moving.

CHARLIE. Lying bastard.

JAKE. Yeah sure come on over . . . (*To* CHARLIE.) Jesus I am made man, she wants to join me.

CHARLIE. Jesus I can feel my tongue tying itself in a knot . . . I'm away over to the riggers . . . I smell a waft of whacki backi comin' from that corner . . .

JAKE. Ah no man, don't leave me on my own.

CHARLIE. Big lad like you scared of a woman.

JAKE. She's not just a woman, she is Caroline Giovanni.

CHARLIE. Here she comes, I'm off . . . (*Stops . . . takes the script from his pocket.*) Just leave that sitting there . . . okay . . . don't be pushy just leave it where she can see it.

CAROLINE. You are in the movie then?

JAKE. Yeah . . . Jake Quinn . . . I'm just one of the crowd.

CAROLINE. I haven't seen you around.

JAKE. I was in that scene the day, you know when you talk to the peasants about asking your father to give the land back.

CAROLINE. I didn't notice anyone I was so uptight about my accent . . . was it alright?

JAKE. You would think you were born here.

CAROLINE. Are you local?

JAKE. Down the road.

CAROLINE. Your countryside is so beautiful.

JAKE. Yeah, you appreciate it more when you have been away . . . I was in the States for a couple of years.

CAROLINE (*not really interested*). Yeah, what part.

JAKE. New York . . . I travelled around as well, I went . . .

CAROLINE. You are enjoying the movie.

JAKE. Yeah it's . . . well different . . . I would like to get into movies proper like.

CAROLINE. You have a great face . . . great eyes . . . the camera would love you.

JAKE. It certainly loves you . . . your last movie was brilliant . . .

CAROLINE. This place is a bit crowded, would you like to come back to the hotel for a drink.

JAKE. I don't think I would be allowed.

CAROLINE. Who would stop you?

JAKE. Well we were warned not to bother you.

CAROLINE. No you were warned not to bother me unless I choose to be bothered and tonight I want you to come for a drink . . . (*Calls.*) Jock will you go get the car, I want to go back to the hotel . . . (*To* JAKE.) Would you like to travel with us.

JAKE. Yeah sure . . . (*Looks up.*) Ah well done Bridget . . . egg and onion.

CAROLINE. See you at the front door then.

JAKE. I think you should have your sandwich first.

CAROLINE. God no, I never eat after six o'clock.

JAKE. Could you pretend and take it with you?

CAROLINE. Why?

JAKE. Because this is a small town and I will get the blame if you don't.

CAROLINE *moves away.*

. . . would you like this?

CHARLIE (*delighted*). She gave me a sandwich.

JAKE. She is driving me to the hotel for a drink . . . I am going with her in the car.

CHARLIE. Jesus man you're made . . . did she notice the script?

JAKE. What did I tell you Charlie, it's who you know in this business.

CHARLIE. Tell her there could be a big part in it for her . . . brilliant death scene . . .

JAKE. Sorry Charlie, Every man for himself.

CHARLIE. Take it with you, just in case.

JAKE. Aye, all right. See ya.

DAVE, *a Cockney, approaches* CHARLIE.

DAVE. Hey Charlie, fancy a line?

CHARLIE. What?

DAVE. Fancy a line?

CHARLIE. Well I have never acted before but I'll give it a go. What do I have to say?

DAVE. Coke.

CHARLIE. COKE!!

DAVE. Jesus mate, want a loud hailer.

CHARLIE. Sorry . . . you got coke?

DAVE. Yeah.

CHARLIE. Happy days . . . fuck I love the movies.

*Next morning . . . interior . . . changing room . . .*
CHARLIE *is rushing about getting ready, hyper still from the coke the night before . . .* JAKE *enters relaxed . . . whistling to himself.*

CHARLIE *and* JAKE *change into costume.*

CHARLIE. What happened man?

JAKE. I think she was trying to . . . you know . . . seduce me.

CHARLIE. You . . . Jesus she could have any man in the whole country . . . the world for Christ sake . . . or maybe she wanted a bit of rough . . . I know what it is . . . in the movie she bonks a peasant . . . in real life she bonks Kurt Steiner who is pretending he is Rory the peasant . . . but if it were real real life she would be bonking somebody like you, a nobody . . . well did you?

JAKE. I was surrounded by minders . . . pretending they weren't listening. But them boys have eyes and ears in their arse.

CHARLIE. And what did you say to her?

JAKE. I told her I wrote poetry . . . thought that would appeal to her . . . you know the handsome heady Irish poet.

CHARLIE. You write poems?

JAKE. No . . . but I had to think of something that would make me interesting, specially to somebody like her . . . talent is sexy if you have eff all else.

*Flashback . . . romantic music . . .* CAROLINE's *bedroom.*

CAROLINE. Poetry . . . that's fascinating.

JAKE. Yeah.

CAROLINE. Are you published?

JAKE. No . . . well I don't believe in that.

CAROLINE. Really.

JAKE. That cheapens your poetry . . . makes it too accessible . . . then people interpret it and get it wrong.

CAROLINE. Would you recite one of your poems for me?

*Present.*

JAKE. So I picked one of Seamus Heaney's.

CHARLIE. Brilliant . . . and I bet ye she was none the wiser.

JAKE. None.

CHARLIE. Must try that.

*Flashback.*

JAKE. Who blowing up these sparks For their meagre heat, have missed The once-in-a-lifetime portent of the comet's pulsing rose.

CAROLINE. There is no of in the last line.

JAKE. Sorry.

CAROLINE. The once-in-a-lifetime portent, The comet's pulsing rose, there is no of . . . Seamus Heaney.

JAKE (*embarrassed*). Yeah.

CAROLINE. You underestimate me, Jake . . . I'm not just here to exploit the beauty of the land, I love it . . . I know the history and the poets.

JAKE. It always works on Irish girls . . .

CAROLINE. Maybe you should try a more obscure poet.

*Present.*

CHARLIE. Did you, you know . . . up in her room.

JAKE. Give her one? She is sort of untouchable . . . I mean she is Caroline Giovanni . . . so I just left, but I have been invited into her Winnebago for coffee.

CHARLIE. You be careful.

JAKE. What you mean careful?

CHARLIE. Well you don't want to be used like.

JAKE. She could use me any day.

CHARLIE. Then the press get hold of it. You know . . .
Extra Gives Movie Star One in a Caravan . . . know,
like your man Hugh Grant and the prostitute.

JAKE. Made her famous didn't it . . . and it's not a caravan it's a Winnebago.

CHARLIE. Oh excuse me . . . anyway, you go to the caravan and I will sneak up to the window with a
Polaroid . . . Front page of *The Sun* . . . we could be
fartin' through silk.

JAKE. No . . . the mother would kill me.

CHARLIE. Mine too . . . you know being brought up
properly is a shaggin' handicap.

JAKE. Not knowing what you are going to do for the
rest of your life is a bigger one.

CHARLIE. Come on man, we are on a movie . . . guys
would give their left testicle to be where we are . . .
forty quid a day, rubbing shoulders with stars.

JAKE. And then what, when it's over, then what?

CHARLIE. Don't even think about it, we have three
weeks  left . . . tell you what, the riggers are boys to
hang out  with . . . comin' down with coke . . . Jesus
that stuff is magic I was out of my head last night
. . . great job that . . . good money, all the coke you
can sniff . . . what a life . . . did she get a wee

chance to have a wee butchers at my script?

JAKE *brings it out of his pocket . . . obviously had forgotten.*

JAKE. Sorry Charlie, just didn't find the right moment.

CHARLIE (*disappointed*). Aye . . . these things have to be timed right . . . it's all in the timing . . . thanks anyway.

AISLING. Quiet everyone . . . settle . . . as soon as you get dressed, please make your way to the minibus immediately where Costume can check you.

CHARLIE (*eager to please*). Right dead on Aisling . . . no problem . . . we are ready . . . I will gee up the rest for you . . . and if you have a wee minute maybe you could have a wee skiff over this . . . I would love you to be involved in it . . .

AISLING (*impatiently*). What?

CHARLIE. My film.

AISLING. Post it to the Production Office . . . come on . . . get a move on.

JAKE. You are pissin' against the wind Charlie.

CHARLIE. No . . . just not quite getting the right moment.

*On the bus.*

CHARLIE. I haven't dug turf since I was a wee buck.

JAKE (*sarcastically*). Yeah it will be a nice romantic rural Irish scene.

CHARLIE. Ack I think it is . . . all us diggin' away at the turf . . . Maeve comin' by on her horse and clockin' Rory and him clockin' her and thinkin' . . . wow I'd love to give her one . . . and all the time the fiddles playing in the background . . . I love the movies. Unreal man.

*Bus stops.*

SIMON. Is there a Jake Quinn here?

JAKE. Yeah.

SIMON (*on walkie talkie to* AISLING). Aisling. Clem's not happy with the cows. The cows. He says they're not Irish enough. I don't know. Black fluffy ones, I suppose. Simon, 1st A.D. Quick word.

JAKE. Sure.

SIMON. Caroline Giovanni wants you to have coffee with her . . . The director has said you can have ten minutes . . . then you will excuse yourself and leave.

JAKE. What if she doesn't want me to leave?

SIMON. Look mate, I am telling you, you have ten minutes, and if you are not out in ten minutes I will come and get you.

CHARLIE (*to* JAKE). Jesus, ten minutes. Ten minutes . . . sure that's more than any of the rest of us would get in a lifetime.

JAKE. Jesus here's the heavy.

JOCK (*big Scottish heavy*). You Jake?

JAKE. Aye if you're Tarzan.

JOCK (*not amused*). The name is Jock Campbell . . . Ms Giovanni's security . . . You might have seen me last night in the hotel.

JAKE. No can't say I did.

JOCK. You will have ten minutes . . . I will be outside the door and when you hear me give two raps you will come out . . . I mean ten minutes and not a second more. Wait here!

JAKE. Hold on I didn't ask for this.

CHARLIE. Jesus, a brick shithouse on legs you boyo.

JAKE. Suddenly I am being treated like I'm a potential attacker . . .

CHARLIE. Now see it from their point of view . . . you are a nobody . . . that is a potential security risk, you are an Irish nobody, that is a definite security risk, you are from the arse hole of nowhere in Ireland and you could be I.R.A., major megga security risk.

JAKE. Out to kidnap her.

CHARLIE. Got it in one.

JOCK. Mr Quinn. We have you listed as Ninth Avenue, New York.

JAKE. I am not long back, I haven't changed it yet . . . you see I live here with my mother.

JOCK. When did you arrive back?

JAKE. Couple of weeks ago.

JOCK. And why did you leave America?

JAKE. I was homesick.

JOCK. And what is your mother's address?

JAKE. Listen mate, do me a favour will you . . . go and tell Miss Giovanni, thank you but no thank you . . . tell her I don't like coffee and I hope she is not too offended.

JOCK. You want me to tell her that? You're lucky to get

a second chance Mr Seamus Heaney.

CHARLIE. Jesus . . . who do these people think they effen' well are?

JAKE. Me and my fekking poetry.

CHARLIE. What do you mean?

JAKE. I lied . . . she knew it was Heaney.

CHARLIE. If I had bin you I would have lied to me too . . . well nobody wants to admit to being a dickhead.

SIMON. Jake could I have a quiet word?

JAKE. What Simon . . . alright.

SIMON. I am going to get into terrible trouble if you don't keep that appointment . . . the security check is necessary . . . Ms Giovanni is worth at least six million and if anything were to happen to her . . .

JAKE. Fine, I understand that, just tell her I would not like to put her at risk.

SIMON. Jake . . . it is very important for us to keep the stars happy, she simply requested that she would like you to join her . . . and if you are clean then you should not worry about the security check.

JAKE. I had a parking fine in 1987 I think I would be a

high risk . . . and what is more I object to you lot
checkin' me out, this is an infringement of my priva-
cy.

SIMON. Well if you must go chatting up important people that's the price you pay.

JAKE. Fuck it, she chatted me up.

SIMON. Look mate, don't go thinking you're anything
special. Miss Giovanni has a habit of going ethnic.
Helps her get into the part. I am giving you a quiet
word of warning . . . Ms Giovanni does not like to
be snubbed, particularly by an extra, and it might be
her request that you be removed from the set, so for
your own good . . .

JAKE. That's it Charlie, I am not going . . . no way,
they can sack me if they like.

CHARLIE. Don't worry, just go and pass yourself . . . let
her do all the talking.

JAKE. Look at all the extras, not one of them has tuk
their eyes off me. Just watching and waiting.

CHARLIE. Just jealous. Forty pound a day mate, forty
pound a day and another three weeks and you never
know, she could be your key into the movies.

JOCK. Right, are you coming? You have ten minutes.

CHARLIE. Good luck Jake . . . (*Looks round.*) What are youse all lookin' at, he is only away to give her one, two consenting adults aren't they . . . (*To* CATERER.) I'll take Jake Quinn's baked Alaska . . . because he is having coffee with Caroline . . . yeah, well me and him and Caroline is sort of friends now . . . yes fresh cream on both would be lovely . . . no thanks two helpings is enough . . .

CAROLINE *is discovered in a yoga position centre stage, playing appropriate music.*

CAROLINE. Hi, how are you?

JAKE. Fine.

CAROLINE. Coffee?

JAKE. Yes, please.

CAROLINE. Sugar?

JAKE. Two please.

CAROLINE. Cream?

JAKE. Yes please.

JAKE. I am only allowed ten minutes.

CAROLINE. We have all the time in the world. Your accent is so beautiful . . . do you mind if you could read my lines and I put a tape on.

JAKE. I thought you had one of them professional accent people.

CAROLINE. I have but there is nothing like the real thing . . . and besides you're far better looking . . .

JAKE. Am . . . how would I go about gettin' into the movies, what is the first step?

CAROLINE (*mimics his accent*). How would I go about getting into the movies . . . that's just so beautiful . . . how do I sound?

JAKE. Sounds great.

CAROLINE. Let's start on page seven.

JAKE. How did you get started?

CAROLINE. You don't want to hear about that. This first speech.

JAKE. I mean should I have an agent or something.

CAROLINE (*angry*). You don't want to get into the movies, it's shit, real shit . . . now could you just read this for me.

JAKE. Rory will your people ever accept me . . .

CAROLINE. Don't mumble . . . I need you to articulate

. . . again . . .

JAKE. But Maeve is one of the landed gentry, she wouldn't talk like us anyway.

CAROLINE (*annoyed*). Excuse me?

JAKE. She'd have been educated in England. She'd talk different like.

CAROLINE. No, but she wants to fit in. She always has.

JAKE. Ah yeh, but she wouldn't have mixed with the locals until she started going out with Rory. You wouldn't pick up an accent that quickly.

CAROLINE. Look I don't have time to sit here with you and discuss what my character would and would not do. Can we just read the script?

JAKE. No . . . I think I had better be going . . .

CAROLINE. Your time isn't up yet.

JAKE. I'm sorry. I think it is.

JAKE *makes to leave* . . . CAROLINE *shouts before he can get out.*

CAROLINE. Jock . . . I'm finished with Mr Quinn.

CAROLINE *attempts to say the words.*

CAROLINE. Rory will your people ever accept . . . no
. . . shit . . . Rory . . . Rory . . . fuck. (*Screams.*)
Jock get John in here now.

JAKE (*to* CHARLIE). I feel like shit man, you know,
being used like that.

CHARLIE. So you were just a sex object with an accent.
I did that to a girl once . . . met her on a ferry,
French she was . . .

JAKE. She said the movies are shit.

CHARLIE. She gets six mill a picture and she thinks it
shit, I am gettin' forty smackaronies and I think it's
class.

AISLING. Quiet . . . settle . . . when Maeve approaches
on the horse, everyone stops digging and looks at
her . . .

CHARLIE (*excited*). Oh good Caroline Giovanni is in
our scene.

AISLING. We won't have Maeve in the scene, so the top
of my hand will be your eye line . . . so when the
camera rolls dig until I raise my hand and my hand
will be Maeve approaching on the horse . . . then
you will all look up and stare at her . . . when I drop
my hand you will look to the left and see Rory
approaching Maeve on the horse.

CHARLIE. Oh brilliant, Kurt Steiner is gonna be in it.

AISLING. . . . Now Rory won't be in the scene.

CHARLIE (*quietly*). Fuck sake is anybody working round here, only us.

AISLING. So when you look to the left, Simon's hand will be Rory approaching Maeve on the horse. All right, everyone OK?

CHARLIE. So it us lookin' dispossessed at her hand, pretending it's Maeve on a horse lookin' sorry for us . . . I'm gonna miss all this.

JAKE. What will you do?

CHARLIE (*brings his script out*). Maybe somebody will read this and say . . . Jesus this is brilliant . . . and I tell ye man . . . I will be made . . .

JAKE. Grow up Charlie.

CHARLIE. And what, just keep touring round Ireland waiting for movies?

JAKE. Even that's dying out . . . they have used up most of the forty shades of green by now.

SIMON. Now remember . . . it's dig . . . Hands over here . . . stop . . . my hands over there . . . turn over, speed, make it . . . ready Clem . . . and action.

*Music.*

*They dig . . . stop . . . look up . . . moving their heads as if watching galloping horses and then stop . . . then look the other way doing the same action . . .*

JAKE *starts to laugh . . . then can't control himself.*

SIMON. Cut . . . yes and what is so funny mate?

JAKE. Sorry . . . it's just hard . . . you know her hand being Maeve on a horse and your hand being Rory and . . . (*Laughs.*) sorry.

SIMON. Time is fucking money here mate.

JAKE. Wasn't just me, everybody laughed.

SIMON. Right . . . quiet, we are going to go for this again . . . this time with a bit of feeling. (*Under his breath.*) Bloody extras.

*They repeat the action as before . . .* JAKE *and* CHARLIE *just about control the laughter.*

SIMON. And cut . . . stay in position until we check the gate.

CHARLIE. Hey Jake . . . if you were a movie star, I could be your minder . . . personal manager, line up the women, try them out first so you won't be disappointed, know like the queen has somebody to taste her dinner.

JAKE. What is the commotion over there?

CHARLIE. Where?

JAKE. Fin looks like he's in a terrible state . . . that's his Da with him . . . must be trouble . . . Fin . . . what's the trouble?

FIN. M'Da has brought terrible news Jake . . . Sean Harkin . . . drowned himself this morning. Da says Danny Mackin was up in his top field and saw Sean walk into the water . . . he didn't know if he was coddin' or what for he had all his clothes on. Danny shouted at him and said he saw Sean comin' back out . . . Danny didn't know what to make of it . . . then he saw him walk into the water again and never rise out of it . . . Danny was too far away to do anything but raise the guards . . . when the divers found him . . . his pockets were full of stones . . . he came out of the water to fill his pockets full of stones.

SIMON. And the gate is clear. Let's move on.

*End of Act One.*

## ACT TWO

**JAKE** *enters . . . he is solemn . . . he stands for a second or two before* **CHARLIE** *enters . . .* **CHARLIE** *enters reading his script . . . He sees* **JAKE,** *he walks up to him and touches his arm as if to say he understands.*

**AISLING.** Quiet everyone . . . settle . . . On Action I want you all to cheer Rory as he emerges from the Big House . . . this is very important . . . It is the final scene where Rory is now the owner of the Big House . . . because he has married Maeve and you know he is going to hand back the land to the people. Big smiling faces and real joy . . . remember it's the big Happy Ending. Over to you Simon. Turn over.

**SIMON.** Cheers Aisling, Turn over, Speed, mark it and ACTION.

**AISLING.** Action.

*SFX Music . . . they run forward . . . stop and make weak attempts at the cheer.*

SIMON. Cut . . . Right everybody we are going to go for that take yet again. So . . . Rory has just married Maeve, you know now that he has inherited the land . . . come on for Christ sake show a bit more jubilation . . . You see Rory coming out of the big house, he's now the owner of the big house. You all see him and cheer. (*They cheer.*) Aisling let's show them what they're doing. PLAYBACK!

*The music is played back . . .* AISLING *and* SIMON *demonstrate how it should be done.*

SIMON. Come on if we don't get this we will have cloud cover. Turnover, speed, mark it and ACTION. Don't. (*To* AISLING, *who is about to say 'Action'.*)

*They cheer . . . again weakly.*

SIMON. Cut, Jesus!

CHARLIE. Hard work this morning. C'mon man, snap out of it.

JAKE. Are you alright, Fin.

FIN *is discovered downstage right.*

FIN. Sean always talked about getting out. He hated this place. He used to say to me, you and me, Fin, we'll escape. He always used that word – escape. He wanted to go to America. He wanted to be someone. You know that last film was made here, we were only kids, we all got carried away. Sean used to sit watching them day after day.

SEAN (*twelve years*). Be brilliant to be in that film wouldn't it Fin.

FIN (*twelve years*). You make loads of money.

SEAN. Will we ask can we be in it . . .

FIN. We would have to dress up in them stupid clothes, I wouldn't be seen dead.

SEAN. But maybe they would spot us and . . . you know take us off to America to make our own film . . . you know like McCauley what's his name.

FIN. My Da wouldn't let me go.

SEAN. To be a millionaire?

FIN. No, sure I have to take over the shop.

SEAN. You would rather be a butcher than a millionaire?

FIN. Well no, but my Da . . .

SEAN. Cuttin' up dead meat when you could be a superstar.

FIN. I'll think about it . . . I would have to ask my Da first.

SEAN. I don't, my Da says us boys has to find something to do 'cos well there will be no need for too many farmers . . . hey, where will you get meat if there will be no cows soon?

FIN. No cows . . . don't talk daft . . . where will they all go?

SEAN. I don't know, America . . . all them trucks and caravans and people, the town is going to be dead soon, we have to get into that film.

FIN. My Da won't let me . . . he says the people's heads is gettin' carried away.

SEAN. Your Da is talking bollicks . . . they are paying thirty quid a day . . . I am going to save mine for America.

*Present.*

JAKE. Maybe he looked at me and realised there was no American Dream.

CHARLIE. Come on, some guys make it . . . yer man that owns the hotel, didn't he leave with fifty dollars, then comes back and buys it inside two years.

JAKE. Yeah for every one of him there is fifty who come back without an arse in their trousers.

CLEM, *the Director.*

CLEM. Hi I'm Clem Curtis the Director . . . we are
goin' to have to go for another take on this . . . this
scene is very important . . . this is the final scene in
the movie, so let me explain . . . I know we are
shooting out of sequence and I am aware that not
many of you don't know the story. Hello, hello. (*To*
JAKE, *who's not concentrating.*) . . . So I want you to
imagine that when Rory walks out of that house he
is about to answer all your hopes and dreams, whatever they are . . . Rory has the answer, so that is
what we want to see on your faces . . . we will be
doing some close-ups, so we want to see real fucking ecstasy here.

JAKE. Real fucking ecstasy? Young Sean Harkin has
killed himself yesterday because of real fucking
ecstasy.

CLEM. Take it easy.

JAKE. Sorry . . . it's just . . . I'm sure you understand
that we are finding it hard to jump for joy.

CLEM. Yes we are aware of that and we are very sorry
but we must get this shot right . . . and I am sorry
for the unfortunate use of the word . . . so if you
could give me some joyful animations.

SIMON. Too late Clem, those clouds are about to hit in
five seconds. I think they are here for the rest of the
morning . . . shall I break the extras for an hour and

go for an interior . . . Aisling . . . break the extras.

AISLING. Okay everybody we will pick this shot up again in a hour, so please no-one leave the set . . . At the end of the day I want everyone to go now to costume. It's the big celebration tomorrow in the grounds of the Big House . . . and you will have new costumes so please see wardrobe before you leave.

CHARLIE. Jesus, is it not the funeral the morra Jake?

JAKE. They will have to work round us . . . the whole town will be there.

CHARLIE. Even so, they should stop anyway, mark of respect.

JAKE. It's the least they could do.

CLEM. Right folks we are in total sympathy with you all and we have sent condolences to the family. (*Aside.*) Have we sent condolences? . . . But I am sure you appreciate we have been held up quite a bit with the weather. I am sorry it will be impossible to let you all free for the funeral tomorrow . . . we have a long day with most of you in shot from early morning . . .

MICKEY. We have to pay our last respects . . . he was related to most of us.

CLEM. Tomorrow is a big day for us . . . we have a marquee being transported, truck loads of fresh flowers shipped over from Holland, three catering companies for the wedding feast . . . we must finish by dusk tomorrow.

MICKEY. You will have to stop for the funeral . . . we will all be there.

CHARLIE (*to* JAKE). Excuse me interrupting you Clem, but why don't you just go ahead and do the wedding, only most of the guests leave to go to a funeral in the town. It's only a story . . . this is the movies, can't you do what you want?

CLEM. We are behind schedule, if we don't do the wedding tomorrow and get finished we are fucked.

JAKE. That's life.

CLEM. Do you people realise that each day we film it costs at least a quarter of a million dollars?

MICKEY. Then how come we only get forty pound a day?

CLEM. Jesus.

JAKE. Well said Mickey.

SIMON. Clem let me deal with it.

CLEM. They are all yours Simon . . . just don't come back with a no or the producers are goin' to have my balls.

SIMON. Listen, guys, we are in total sympathy with you . . . but if we cut filming by two hours we would be in real crisis . . . we need that for weather cover. It would be a disaster if we didn't wrap up that scene tomorrow . . . We would have to go into another hire situation for the marquees . . . the producers won't cover us if we run over . . . I am prepared to pay all of you an extra twenty quid.

MICKEY. How much did he say Jake?

JAKE. Not enough Mickey.

SIMON. . . . Guys . . . seriously . . . listen . . . Push comes to shove, we could sack all of you. Remember that.

MICKEY. He can't sack us, we are in the can.

CHARLIE. What's that Mickey?

MICKEY. We're on tape . . . in the camera . . . are you thick . . . it will luk bloody daft in the last scene if the whole lot of us luked like a whole load of other ones wouldn't it. We're in the can, in the camera, on tape – are you thick? . . . The producer may be after his balls, but it's us that has them.

CHARLIE. Jake where are you going . . . we are not allowed to leave the set.

JAKE. We have an hour, I have to go somewhere.

*SFX . . . Classroom bell.*

JAKE. Brother Gerard . . . Hello, Jake Quinn.

BROTHER GERARD. Jake Quinn, sure I remember you well . . . how was America?

JAKE. Fine . . . Brother I want to talk to you about young Sean Harkin.

BROTHER GERARD. A terrible tragedy, terrible for the whole family. He was a grand youngin. I remember his first year.

*Flashback.*

BROTHER GERARD. Cunas, cunas. Sean Harkin come up to the front of the class please. Now Sean here is going to read out his essay on cows . . . come on Sean.

SEAN (*eight years*). Cows are great big useful beasts. They are more useful than humans. They are more useful because you can get meat from them, then you can get milk and butter and they even make good school bags. Cows are the business because many people live off cows and they give you no bother as long as you feed them and milk them. A cow is even useful when it goes to the toilet because we need the manure to fertilise the land. If I were a cow I would feel very useful. I would rather be a dairy cow so that I didn't have to be killed. When I grow up I am going to have the best herd in Kerry.

*Present.*

BROTHER GERARD. Muy hu agus sigi sios. He was a nice child from a good family, then he just got carried away. The father sold off a lot of the land to make ends meet and the kid's hopes went with it. And how are you, Jake – what has brought you back from America?

JAKE. Homesick brother . . . am Sean, was he a kid that got depressed or anything?

BROTHER GERARD. Not a bit of him . . . you couldn't cut him with a bread knife . . . he lived in another world . . . a world he lived out in his head . . . you know imagination can be a damned curse in this country.

JAKE. What did he talk about, what did he want?

BROTHER GERARD. Tell you the truth he was as normal as the rest when it came to that . . . they wanted to be rock stars, film stars, footballers . . . if one of them had said a teacher or a dentist or something I would have dropped dead with the shock . . . problem with Sean was, he was convinced he could be all the things he wanted . . . and at times thought he was.

*SFX . . . School Bell.*

JAKE. Thanks Brother Gerard . . . thanks.

CHARLIE. Hurry up Jake earache was lukin' ye, I said you were at the Jacks.

JAKE. Thanks Charlie, where was I?

CHARLIE. You were standin' here.

SIMON. Aisling, change of plan. Light's perfect for the eviction scene.

AISLING. Great Simon. The natives are a bit restless, I think we should go for it quickly.

SIMON (*speaks into his walkie talkie*). Good girl. Right . . . fine Clem . . . I'll tell them . . . Quiet . . . Ms Giovanni would like to talk to you all for a moment, so don't leave your positions until she comes.

JAKE. Do we get on our knees.

CHARLIE. Give it a rest.

CAROLINE. Look, I am really sorry about what has happened . . . I know you are a small neighbourhood and everyone is greatly affected by it . . . it's such a terrible tragedy . . . I just want you all to know that I appreciate you all being here and carrying on under such sad circumstances . . . thank you . . . and well . . . just thank you.

CHARLIE *claps and encourages others.*

CHARLIE. Now that was very nice of her, she didn't have to do that.

JAKE. Know what gets me Charlie . . . these people think that it has nothing to do with them.

CHARLIE. It hasn't.

JAKE. Of course it has, terrible tragedy, I'll tell you what's a terrible tragedy, filling young Sean's head with dreams.

CHARLIE. No different from me that kid . . . like all of us . . . like you, don't *we* dream, do you not fantasise about being the cock of the walk, the boy in the big picture . . . like, why couldn't it happen to us if it happens to other people . . . eh? Do you never get carried away into that other world . . . we are no different.

JAKE. Except that we are still alive.

AISLING. Quiet everyone, settle . . . when you are ready we will do the eviction scene . . . that is, Rory and his family being evicted . . . The bailiffs gallop on, they dismount, go into the house. They eject the furniture first and then the people . . . No no. It is a silent scene . . . no angry abuse . . . you are defeated men . . . so watch in silence.

JAKE (*to* CHARLIE). Aye dead on . . . did you ever, as if all us would stand by and watch a whole family being evicted without opening our mouths . . . even if it was just . . . go on you rotten bastards, just something. Defeated broken men . . .

JAKE. Oh that's no problem . . . Typecast.

CHARLIE (*to* JAKE). Not yet . . . (*Brings the script out of his pocket.*) If only I could get one person to read this. You know they tell the rest . . . and it snowballs. That's how it happened.

JAKE. Charlie you know as well as I do if that script ever gets into one of their hands it will hit the bottom of a waste basket and never see the light of day again.

CHARLIE. Look I don't need this kind of negative shit, do ya hear.

JAKE. Then get real . . . Charlie . . .

CHARLIE. Excuse me . . . this is real . . .

JAKE. And what if they say you have written a load a bollicks and you'll never make nothing writing shit like that . . . then what?

CHARLIE. I won't believe them.

JAKE. You will Charlie, and you know it.

SIMON. OK. We're going to go for this now. Remember you're defeated, broken men. Turnover, Speed, mark it, and ACTION. OK Clem.

*They enact eviction as detailed by* AISLING.

Lovely . . . and we will check the gate . . . if the gate is clear that is a wrap . . . do you hear . . . quiet . . . that is a wrap for the night . . . check your calls for the morning . . . goodnight and pray for sun tomorrow or we are all in big trouble.

*They take their extra clothes off.*

MICKEY. That Simon fella's off his head, rain hail snow, we still get our forty quid.

CHARLIE. What about the funeral? Are they stopping to let us go to the funeral?

MICKEY. No choice we put our futs down . . . power to the people eh Jake . . . they say they will get it all done only if we have sunshine for eight hours . . . I puts my hand up like this to the wind, you see? . . .

and then I gets down on the ground and I listens to the earth and then I tuk my hat off and threw it up to see what way it would land and it landed the right way up, so I says . . . it will be a scorcher, you won't see a cloud next or near the place . . . and that convinced him.

CHARLIE. That's amazing.

MICKEY. A pity it's a load of bollicks . . . here's the forty quid man comin', now that is what I call a ray of sunshine, Dermot.

*They change into clothes.*

JAKE. See you, Mickey. See you later. Charlie, I will take you to Sean's wake the night.

CHARLIE. But I never knew him.

JAKE. Won't matter . . . you're with me . . . hey I'm sorry for earlier.

CHARLIE. It's alright . . . I understand . . .

JAKE. I shouldn't get on to you . . . at least you're trying to do somethin' with your script . . . Mickey has watched his whole way of life fall apart around him . . . and now all it's worth is a backdrop for an American movie . . . he depends on their forty quid a day and then he lives in hope for the next one . . . he's some boy, he never lets it get to him.

*LX . . . change.*

JAKE. Mr Harkin . . . sorry for your trouble . . . Charlie Conlon, he's on the film.

MR HARKIN. Hello Charlie . . .

JAKE. Terrible tragedy, Mr Harkin.

MR HARKIN. Aye . . . go on in there Jake. I'll see you after the milkin' . . . rain hail or death the cows haft to be milked . . .

JAKE. Sure, I'll do that for you.

MR HARKIN. No, you're all right Jake, all Sean ever knew as a young one was the land . . . same as you Jake, aah he looked up to you . . . I didn't know what to say to him when the land had let him down . . . anyway, go on into the house, there is a feed and a bit of music . . . I can give Sean nothin' more now but a dacent wake . . . I will see you after milkin'.

*The Wake.*

CHARLIE *and* JAKE *as if in a room full of people . . . SFX traditional music.*

CHARLIE. Sorry for your trouble. I'm Charlie Conlon – a friend of Jake's.

JAKE. How's it goin' Malachy? . . . alright Mary? How ya Fin?

CHARLIE. How are you doin' . . . hello . . . it's like being on the set . . . the same people.

JAKE. Hello Paddy . . . Aye it's tough being in the movies.

CHARLIE. Great music.

JAKE. The family are all traditional players.

MICKEY. He is gettin' a great send off . . . some of the best players in Ireland.

JAKE. Do you not play yourself then Mickey?

MICKEY. I will get a few more gargles in me and I will see if the oul squeeze box will loosen up.

JAKE. How's it's goin' Fin? . . .

*Takes* FIN *aside.*

FIN. Jake, everything he wanted was somewhere else . . . he hated this town. He said it let him down . . . everybody let him down . . . but sure that couldn't be helped . . . that's the way it was and nobody's fault . . . you know some of us just accepted that life wasn't great, but he wouldn't . . . he stopped going out he just got his gear and stayed in his room with his movies . . . virtual reality. That kept him going, drugs and movies.

JAKE. What was it about that day? Why was it different from any other?

FIN. He had tried to get on the movie the day before but he was out of his head . . . Then, that night in the pub . . . they were all there . . . all arse lickin' the yanks it seemed he was right in the middle of the world he fantasised about . . . you know, the beautiful American star, the movies. He knew the crew had coke . . . they were all laughin' and joking and he just watched them and then he tried to score. He saw your woman talking to you and then he went up to her . . .

*Flashback.*

SEAN *staggers over to* CAROLINE.

SEAN. Caroline . . . you are Caroline Giovanni.

CAROLINE (*panics*). Go away.

SEAN. I only want to say hello, I am Sean Harkin.

CAROLINE. Get away from me.

SEAN. I won't touch you I just want to look at you.

CAROLINE. Jock . . . Jock . . . I am being pestered, get rid of him.

JOCK (*grabs him*). Right you out, if I see you back in here I will break your two fuking legs.

*Present.*

FIN. He was put out on the street, out of the pub in his own town . . . he sat outside on the street, I went with him.

JAKE. And then he watched me go off with her didn't he?

FIN. Yeah.

JAKE. And what did he say?

FIN. Nothing.

JAKE. What did he say . . . tell me?

FIN. I said he didn't say anything.

JAKE. He must have said something.

FIN. Waster . . . fukin' waster Fin . . . what is she doing with a waster like Jake Quinn . . . that's what he said.

JAKE. Jesus, Charlie.

CHARLIE. It's not your fault . . . not one person is to blame.

JAKE. . . . I have to get out of here . . .

SIMON *is about to have a nervous breakdown . . .*

SIMON (*on walkie talkie*). I don't fuckin' believe this . . . two truck loads of flowers and we have to scrap them . . . can he not take shaggin' pills like anybody else . . . Jesus . . . right . . . right . . . Aisling . . . Aisling.

AISLING. Aisling here Simon.

SIMON. Aisling we are going for an exterior . . . Kurt has hay fever and wants the flowers scrapped from the marquee . . . Jesus . . . two effing trucks of effing flowers.

AISLING. Oh no . . . can we send them back?

SIMON. Yeah, they'll be dead by the time they hit Holland. This is a nightmare, it took four hours to put them in for that wanker to tell us he had shaggin' hay fever TURN THAT MUSIC OFF . . . set up for the exterior street dance.

AISLING. Copy that Simon.

JAKE. Hey fella, if you have flowers now they won't go to waste, young Sean Harkin's funeral today.

SIMON. It's not up to me . . . and I can tell you by the time they get through to America and get a producer to ask another producer to ask the executive producer the young fella will be dead and buried a week and we will have a shit load of dead flowers to dump . . . Jesus I am crackin' up.

CAROLINE. Excuse me Simon . . . Jake that is very touching and of course the flowers will be delivered to the Chapel . . . Simon see to it immediately. Whatever the cost I will attend to it.

JAKE (*sourly*). Thanks.

CAROLINE. I am really sorry, it must be so hard for you.

JAKE. Yes it is . . . very hard . . . and more so when I think of the way I treated him, the way you and everybody else treated him like he was a piece of muck on their boots.

CAROLINE. Excuse me? . . . I didn't even know him.

JAKE. No, but you had him thrown out of the pub, in his own town in front of his own people, think about that for humiliation . . . think about what that did to his self esteem.

CAROLINE. I don't know what you're talking about.

JAKE. Course you don't, you come here and use us, use

the place and then clear off and think about nothing you leave behind.

CAROLINE. Listen here, I work hard in this industry, I have worked for everything I have ever done, I have used nobody.

JAKE. Yeah well maybe this industry that you work so hard for might be one of the things that drove that kid to do what he did.

CAROLINE. Don't be ridiculous.

JAKE. You're right, I am being called now to dance up and down the street for the big happy ending. Yes I feel ridiculous.

*He walks away . . .* CAROLINE *stands a moment . . . then leaves.*

*Music.* CHARLIE *and* JAKE *dance as if with other people.*

SIMON. Cut . . . beautiful . . . the Irish know one thing, it's how to dance.

CHARLIE. You would think he wasn't Irish.

JAKE. He just wishes he wasn't.

SIMON. Yeah mate you're right, because every time you fuck up I get it in the ear from these people . . . ever

hear the phrase . . . Irish what do you expect . . .
well unfortunately for me they tend to include the
whole nation . . . (*To his walkie talkie.*) Aisling
break the extras for the funeral . . . they have an
hour and a half . . . tell them anybody that comes
back smelling of alcohol will be put off the set.

MICKEY. Holy mother a Jasis, a funeral without a drink
. . . never heard of it happening in my life and I
have bin to more funerals than the undertaker himself . . . a dry funeral in Kerry, what is happening to
the world?

JAKE *and* CHARLIE *stand face front as if in the
Chapel.* CHARLIE *is sneezing.*

*SFX organ music.*

CHARLIE. Bloody flowers . . . I suppose it doesn't matter about my hayfever does it . . .

JAKE. How can she do that . . . she let them walk her
up to the front pew . . . she didn't even know him
. . . she had him thrown out of the pub like a piece
of dirt . . . bitch.

CHARLIE. She paid for the flowers that's why . . .
Anyway it's nice for the family . . . come on settle
yourself, don't blame her . . . she didn't know the
kid was going to kill himself.

JAKE. . . . I am so fucking . . .

CHARLIE. Stop it.

JAKE. Just don't know what to do . . . it's not with her, not with anybody on the film. It's . . .

CHARLIE (*sneezes*). Do you mind, but I am moving to another pew . . . friggin' flowers . . .

CHARLIE *moves away.*

CAROLINE *being interviewed.*

INTERVIEWER. Ms Giovanni has this tragedy affected the filming of *Quiet Valley*?

CAROLINE. As you can see most of the cast and crew are here to pay our last respects . . . so yes it has, but the people are so strong and resilient and have elected to continue filming this afternoon.

INTERVIEWER. Miss Giovanni. Did you know Sean Harkin . . .

CAROLINE. I didn't but from what I hear he was a well loved son and friend . . . we are all very shocked by the events. I just want to get my car please.

INTERVIEWER. I believe he wanted to be an extra on the movie.

CAROLINE. I wouldn't know about that . . . (*Walks away.*) Jock I'm ready.

INTERVIEWER *goes after her.*

INTERVIEWER. And what do you think of Ireland.

CAROLINE. Oh it is so magical . . . the country is so dramatic.

INTERVIEWER. And when can we expect to see *The Quiet Valley*?

CAROLINE. Next year I would imagine.

INTERVIEWER. Well the whole country will be looking forward to it and thank you Ms Giovanni . . . (*Turns front.*) Kevin Doherty for R. T. E. in County Kerry.

*Marquee music.*

SIMON. That's fine for level, thanks. Could we have everyone in the marquees, we have set up and we want to get the interiors done . . . it will be long and slow so be prepared.

CHARLIE. Be prepared that's me Simon. Dib dib I was in the Brownies.

JAKE. What is it with you Charlie eh . . . every time I say something that might need a bit of serious head stuff, you walk away.

CHARLIE. What are you on about?

JAKE. In the chapel . . . you walked away from me.

CHARLIE. Hayfever.

JAKE. No that's just another excuse not to take on the real world . . . you change the subject, tell a stupid joke . . . what is going on behind that bloody annoying cheerful chappie eh . . . you can't be Mr Clown all the time.

CHARLIE. What . . . who says I can't . . . oh you want me to be like Matt Talbot, batin' myself up, that would suit you would it?

JAKE. No . . . just want to know what makes you tick.

CHARLIE. None of your business.

JAKE. You have nothing in your life you are going nowhere and why is it doing my head in and not yours . . . what is going on, I need to know?

CHARLIE. Who says I am going nowhere . . . I have done somethin' . . . I have my script . . . I have something.

JAKE. Read your script . . . it is the biggest load of oul bollicks I have ever read in my life.

CHARLIE (*sits on the ground*). Bastard . . . why are you hurting me? I never do that to you . . . why are you doing this?

JAKE. Charlie, it's every bad film you have ever seen, no story, cardboard people . . . I suppose it's based on real life experience . . . is the Hero you the one that goes in search of the baddies and blows them away . . . like Sean? Wake up for Christ sake.

CHARLIE. And what, be like you, walkin' around hatin' everything, everybody, lookin' for reasons to blame the world.

JAKE. I don't need to look for reasons, I look round me and so should you.

CHARLIE. Sean again is it? You are trying to use that kid to try to justify your own miserable existence . . . you want it to be your fault, you want to be able to say that kid died because of me . . . no, believe me, you're not that fucking important.

JAKE. I could have gave him hope.

CHARLIE. You couldn't have give him nothing,

JAKE. I could!

CHARLIE. No you couldn't. It was too late.

JAKE. It wasn't.

CHARLIE. It was . . . I know I was where Sean was I woke up one morning and looked around me and I saw nothing . . . a big black hole of nothin' . . . and I wanted to jump into that big black hole as far down it as I could get, so I wouldn't have to wake up another morning . . . and when I woke up in the hospital, you know what I thought, my first thought . . . Charlie you are a pathetic bastard, you couldn't even do that right.

JAKE. Charlie . . . sorry . . . sorry mate.

CHARLIE. It's alright, it's just the day that's in it, the kid being buried, people are just over-emotional . . . ignore me . . .

JAKE. Charlie, sorry what I said about the film . . . I'll read it again.

CHARLIE. Nah, you are probably right . . . deep down I knew it was bollicks . . .

AISLING. Alright you two – into the marquee at once, less of the chit chat . . . the tables have been laid out as a banquet . . . I want no one touching the food until we have a take . . .

SIMON. Aisling, Aisling, get that drunken old bollicks off the set now. Clem is about to throw a wobbler . . . I said now . . . he has just knocked over a trestle table full of drinks . . . move him . . . (*On walkie talkie.*) Get me security. Why not. It's OK, I'll take care of it myself – OK you, you had your fun, now move.

MICKEY (*drunk*). They can't sack me I am in the can,
Jake . . . they can't sack me, the last laugh is on me
Mickey Riordain . . .

(*Sings.*)
When all beside a vigil keep, the West asleep
The West asleep Alas and well my Aisling weep
When Connaught lies in slumber deep
There lakes and plain smile fair and free
Mid Rocks their guardian chivalry.

SIMON. For Christ sake . . . (*To* MICKEY.) Right you,
you were warned . . . move it.

MICKEY. You can't sack me, I am in the can.

SIMON. There are three hundred and fifty of you in the
can . . . nobody is even going to notice, now move it
and don't come back.

MICKEY. You can't sack me . . . I am the only surviving extra on *The Quiet Man*, you can't sack me.

SIMON. Move or we will call the police.

MICKEY. You see this ground you are standing on ya
jumped up gobshite, this belonged to my
Grandfather, and you are telling me a Riordan to get
off my land . . . what is happening to the world Jake,
what is happening to the shaggin' world.

SIMON. Aisling call the guards will you, there is going

to be trouble. This oul bollicks won't leave.

MICKEY. No . . . there's no need, yous had young Sean Harkin put out onto the street in his own town and you are not going to do that to me.

JAKE. Don't go, Mickey stay . . . you never let nothing beat ya Mickey, stay.

MICKEY. I will go of my own free will . . . in fact I resign.

Sing oh, let man learn liberty
From crashing wind and lashing sea.

*Straightens himself . . . holds his head up.*

CHARLIE. Jake . . . let him go, don't start. I can't take no more of this . . . I am going into this marquee now, I am doing what is asked of, I'm keeping my head down and that's that so don't fucking start because I don't want to hear no more.

JAKE. Charlie wait.

CHARLIE. I said knock it on the head.

JAKE. No listen, remember what you said earlier when the Director wasn't going to stop for the funeral, you said, sure stick it in the film, this is the movies you can do what you want . . . You are right Charlie, it's only a story . . . if it was a story about a film being made and a young lad commits suicide . . . in other words the stars become the extras and the extras become the stars . . . so it becomes Sean's story, and Mickey and all the people of this town.

CHARLIE. Yes and . . .

JAKE. Why couldn't it be done, don't we have the right to tell our story, the way we want it.

CHARLIE. We could tell it 'til the cows come home but would that . . .

JAKE (*excited*). Yes cows . . . that's it . . . that's where it starts . . . Brilliant Charlie . . . the cows are where it starts and finishes . . . as he walked into the water to die the last thing he would have seen were the cows, the cows that should have been his future in the field looking at him . . . what do you say Charlie . . .

CHARLIE. What, you mean we do this movie?

JAKE. Why not, eh, we have just witnessed it all, haven't we . . . you have been where Sean was, you could get into his head better than anybody . . . you can write a script.

CHARLIE. A script . . . you told me it was a load o' bollicks.

JAKE. Yeah the story was, but you did it . . . you sat

down and did it.

CHARLIE. Who is gonna listen to the likes of us?

JAKE. Well you must have thought somebody was gonna read your script. Otherwise why were you shuvin' it up everybody's nose?

CHARLIE. I knew they wouldn't . . . isn't that pathetic . . . I knew nobody would read it.

JAKE. You are full of shit man.

CHARLIE. You say that to me again and I will swing for you . . . Mister hate the world . . . I can't take any more knocks . . . do you hear . . . no more.

JAKE. Sorry Charlie, sorry, alright I understand . . . I do
. . . Charlie it's just . . . how do I put this . . . Charlie, you and me are fucked, we have nothing, and we are going nowhere, but for the first time in my life I feel I can do something . . . they can only knock us if we don't believe in ourselves . . . and I believe this could work Charlie I do . . . Please give it a go, we have nothing to lose, no money no reputation, no assets.

CHARLIE (*indignant*). I have a tent.

JAKE. That's it. Canvas Productions.

CHARLIE. What?

JAKE. Thanks Charlie.

CHARLIE. Hey stall the ball there I never . . .

JAKE. We have the story, we go to one of these people here and say, tell us where to go from here . . . they all started somewhere.

CHARLIE. They're all too busy clawing their way up to the top to stop and listen to us.

JAKE. Tomorrow at breakfast we get yer man Clem the director . . . he sits over on his own and has his breakfast . . .

CHARLIE. Well, what do we say to him?

JAKE. Tonight we plan out our strategy in our Production Office.

CHARLIE. Wha?

JAKE. In the tent . . . Canvas Productions . . . float it on the Stock Market.

CHARLIE. Yeah and if it rains we will be floatin' with it.

CLEM *is munching his breakfast and thinking.*

JAKE. So the last image you see is Sean, going into the

water and the cows watching him . . . the cows that should have been his future, watching him as he drowns.

JAKE. Well Clem, what do you think?

CLEM. It's just not sexy enough.

JAKE. What . . . what do ya mean?

CLEM. What if the Kid was pursued by Drug Pushers.

JAKE. But he wasn't.

CLEM. Movies aren't real life . . . excuse me for a second . . . (*He speaks into his walkie talkie.*) Aisling sweetheart could you bring me some more coffee . . . no sugar, watching the figure . . . you're a gem . . . (*To* JAKE.) Where was I . . . Oh yes . . . you are going to need a love interest.

JAKE. He loved the land . . . his cows.

CLEM (*winces*). Oh I've got a good idea, what if Fin was a girl . . . the girlfriend who tried to keep him straight.

CHARLIE. But Fin was his mate, he was all Sean had, he couldn't keep a relationship with a girl.

CLEM. Well I am only trying to tell you, you won't move it unless you are aware of these elements . . .

thank you Aisling, you are an angel . . . are we set up for the first shot?

AISLING. Almost there Clem.

CLEM. Good, give me a shout I won't be long . . . look boys why don't you take it to the Irish Film Board?

JAKE. But this could happen to any kid, any rural kid.

CLEM. Sure, but it's not commercial enough. How many people want to see a film about a suicide? People want happy endings. Life is tough enough. People don't go to the movies to get depressed.

CHARLIE. How can you have a happy ending about a kid who drowns himself?

CLEM. He doesn't.

JAKE. But he did.

CLEM. No . . . the farmer who sees him walk into the water actually saves him . . . just in time.

JAKE. And then what?

CLEM. Well . . . that's the end.

AISLING. We're ready for you now Clem.

CLEM. Super . . . must go . . . oh by the way do you have a title for it?

**JAKE.** Yeah . . . *Stones in His Pockets.*

**CLEM.** What do you think of that Aisling, as a title for a movie.

**AISLING.** Doesn't say much . . . not very catchy . . . a bit nondescript.

**CLEM.** This girl is learning well . . . right Aisling let's move.

**CHARLIE.** First knock back . . . and Canvas Productions was only launched last night . . . that must be a record.

**JAKE.** Do you think they are right?

**CHARLIE.** No . . . No . . . Jake . . . I don't.

**JAKE.** Jesus . . . neither do I . . . god. All the time he was talking I kept saying to myself you are wrong . . . Charlie for the first time in my life I believed me.

**CHARLIE.** I'm so used to believing everything I do is bound to be no good.

**JAKE.** Not this time Charlie.

**CHARLIE.** No . . . not this time.

**JAKE.** So you have the opening scene of the film, people comin' onto the land to ask Mr Harkin can they shoot over the landscape . . . but we see it from the kids' point of view and him a wee buck.

CHARLIE. So all you see is cows, every inch of screen, cows . . . cows, just cows and in the middle of it all these trendy designer trainers.

JAKE. Like Aisling's?

CHARLIE. Exactly, sinkin' into a a big mound of steaming cow clap . . . this is the first thing this child sees, the first intrusion into his world.

JAKE. Yeah . . . Cows . . . big slabbery dribblin' cows.

JAKE *and* CHARLIE . . . *animated.*

JAKE. Udders, tails, arses, in your face.

CHARLIE. Fartin', atin', dungin' . . . mooin'.

JAKE. Big dirty fat brutes . . . lukin' at ye . . . wide shots.

CHARLIE. Yes, mid shots.

JAKE. Yes. Close ups.

BOTH. Yes.

*Blackout*

*The End.*

MARIE JONES

Born in Belfast, Marie Jones was writer-in-residence there for
Charabanc Theatre Company from 1983 to 1990. Plays written
for Charabanc include *Lay up Your Ends* (co-written with Martin
Lynch); *Oul Delph* and *False Teeth; Now You're Talking; Girls in
the Big Picture; Somewhere over the Balcony; The Hamster
Wheel* (published in *The Crack in the Emerald:* NHB); *The
Terrible Twins' Crazy Christmas; The Blind Fiddler of
Glenadauch; Weddins, Weeins and Wakes* and *Gold in the Streets.*
Marie has written several plays for Replay Productions and
DubbelJoint Theatre Company. Plays for Replay include *Under
Napoleon's Nose; Hiring Days; Don't Look Down; Yours Truly;
The Cow, the Ship and the Indian* and *It's a Waste of Time Tracy.*
For DubbelJoint, plays include *Hang All the Harpers* (co-written
with Shane Connaughton); *The Government Inspector* (adapta-
tion); *A Night in November; Women on the Verge of HRT* and
*Stones in His Pockets.* The last two went on to enjoy successful
runs in the West End of London. Her most recent plays are
*Women on the Verge Get a Life*, which toured the UK and *Ruby,*
which opened in Belfast in 2000, about the life of the singer Ruby
Murray.

Marie has also written various pieces for both TV and radio and is
the recipient of the John Hewitt Award for Contribution to
Cultural Traditions.

*Stones in His Pockets* won the Irish Times/ESB Award for best
production of 1999. In London it recently won the Evening
Standard Award for Best Comedy and the Olivier Award for Best
New Comedy.